Wires Over the Homeplace

Molly
Thanks for coming and
good luck in your
work.
[illegible]

Also by
Paul Dickey

What Wisconsin Took

They Say This is How Death Came Into the World

Liberal Limericks of 2012

The Good News According to St. Dude: A Play in Two Acts

Wires Over the Homeplace

POEMS BY

PAUL DICKEY

PINYON PUBLISHING
Montrose, Colorado

Book and Cover Design by Susan E. Elliott

Photograph of Paul Dickey by Melissa Mallon

First Edition: September 2013

Pinyon Publishing
23847 V66 Trail, Montrose, CO 81403
www.pinyon-publishing.com

Library of Congress Control Number: 2013946777
ISBN: 978-1-936671-20-5

Acknowledgments

Many of the poems previously appeared in the following journals:

"A Knack for Losing Things." *Rattle*, no. 32, 2009.

"Breaking Into Unlocked Hearts." *Avatar Review* 6, 2004.

"Coming Home To See Dad" and "Family Farm Tomorrow at Public Auction." *2River View* 8, no. 3, 2004.

"Dean's Tree Service." *Valparaiso Poetry Review* 14, no. 2, 2013.

"Departure" *42opus* 4, no. 3, 2004.

"Failed Portrait of the Artist's Daughter" and "Reno County, Kansas Church Cemetery." *2River View* 14, no.1, 2009.

"Frontier Ancestors," "Holiday," and "The Radio in Wartime." *Pinyon Review,* no. 2, 2012.

"Girl in Bikini, By the Water's Edge." *Rattle* 21, 2004.

"How the Lovers Became Different." *Concho River Review* 18, no. 1, 2004.

"How to Decorate a Closet," "How They Once Were," and "On the State Line." *Softblow,* October 2011.

"Happiness and Sadness You Will Not Have With You Always." *Plainsongs,* 26, no. 1, 2005.

"Hymns Sung For the Obvious." *Anti-*, no. 9, 2011.

"I Don't Know How She Learned of Sadness." *Ascent,* November 2012.

"(It Could) Have Gone Either Way" and "For a Time." *Barnwood,* September 2011.

"Incident near O'Neill, Nebraska," "Instructions for Buying a Loaf of Bread," and "Soldier Left in the Sand." *Otoliths,* no. 25, 2012.

"It Will Be Exactly Like Something I Do Not Know." *Nidus*, no. 6, 2004.

"Lazarus, Visiting Kansas." *Diode* 5, no. 3, 2012.

"Pebbles." *32 Poems* 10, no. 2, 2012.

"Potted Plant." *Kansas Quarterly* 12, no. 1, 1980.

"Rick of Firewood Out Back, Behind the Nursing Home." *Prime Number,* September 2011.

"Shoppers." *Ascent,* December 2011.

"Sister Lyons and the Gospel." *Concho River Review,* Fall/ Winter 2011.

"Sliding House. *Foundling Review,* Spring 2013.

"Tea and Coffee." *Hampden-Sydney Poetry Review*, no. 38, 2012.

"The Awards Ceremony" and "Design." *Diode* 5, no. 3, 2012.

"Theories of Family." *Concho River Review,* Fall 2012.

"The Night My Father and I Lost Each Other." *Nimrod* 21, no. 1, 1976.

"The Old-Time Hardware Store." *Midwest Quarterly* 52, no. 4, 2011.

"This P-em Cant Even Fix the Leaky Faucet" and "The Men's Hot Tub and the Fear of the Unknown." *Otoliths,* no. 28, 2013.

"The Season of Almost" and "Woods Interior." *Otoliths,* no. 29, 2013.

"Walking on Water." *qarrtsiluni,* May-June 2008.

"We Never Know." *Prairie Schooner* 86, no. 2, 2012.

"What Wisconsin Took." *Cider Press Review* 4, 2005.

For Willyne

CONTENTS

i. Frontier Ancestors

ii. A Knack For Losing Things

iii. We Never Know

i. Frontier Ancestors

FRONTIER ANCESTORS

The old Indians have told me, that the white men first came from the foam of the ocean, thrown up upon the beach. After laying for a time, subjected to the heat of the sun, they assumed the human form, and walked forth into the interior of the country.

—Coacoochee, Seminole War Chief, taken captive by the U.S. Army while negotiating under a flag of truce in 1837

I carried an old Pennsylvania long rifle into the woods where the remnants of Indian tribes still mingled to threaten my grandfathers. I looked at the old chief intently—into his deeply scarred face of many rivers and the high cheek bones of old mountains. I asked him why. Why had he not given up? Why would he not leave us alone? We meant well even if by chance we had questioned his old ways. We had lived in the Scottish lowlands for generations and had lost everything in Ireland. Even our own father's lands. Surely he could understand that. I debated with him. His ancestors had been here thousands of years and surely they had enough of this land that would soon only be an inhospitable Pittsburgh, blue collar hills, and factories. Surely he knew a better land where his people would thrive, lands where they could rediscover their own ancient traditions. In the bountiful land we were starting to call America. But of course, I knew his answer. He stared back as if I were a fool and had no heart. Perhaps he felt sorry for me. A smoking pipe dangled from his leather belt—made from his own hides but in a trading post somewhere this side of the Philadelphia seaport. Smoke from log cabins, dreams, and family enveloped the frontier and began to drift into Ohio and Illinois, and at last, Iowa and Oklahoma.

POTTED PLANT

In the waiting room, Dad and I
lit cigarettes, held the smoke
in the heart, not telling

a soul. Near the county
school Dad taught, near the family
wheat lands, every blade

was in the hands of God.
All afternoon, we read
the torn magazines.

Dad thumbed
a two-year old Sports Illustrated.
Tares grew into our voices.

Blackbirds perched on the wires
over the homeplace,
eavesdropped on the anonymous

snowflakes I breathed
to my sister over the phone:
Tonight, Mom goes into extra innings.

Now the doctor says to go up.
Dad carries a potted plant, as though
a Willie Mays made the catch.

IT WILL BE EXACTLY LIKE SOMETHING I DO NOT KNOW

I have come from nowhere,
bearing the full baggage of history,
stowing the ancient instruments
that no more predict the future—
to where the rivers part,

and morning replaces midnight
and midnight replaces morning.
I do not know old lovers anymore.
We said goodbye in the old world,
and I live with them in the new.

We greet the strangers with loyalty.
They waited for me, I want,
with jobs. Their whims and laughter
put us up for the night.
I have crossed the ocean

with all my valuables, my sweat.
I print on the documents
in the strange language, so my grandsons
will have the same name as my brothers.
Years from now, a man resembling me,

will stand at the elderberry tree.
He must decide if to chop it down,
or to give it another season.
He will be old and no right
or wrong to the matter. Not even then.

HOW DICKEYVILLE, WISCONSIN MIGHT HAVE GOTTEN ITS NAME

I tell my wife as we drive up highway 35 from Dubuque:
my great-great-grandfather, a Scots-Irish
Indian-fighter, War of 1812 veteran, started a church here.
I talk to myself: did Grandma tell me this,
or did I make it all up? I remind myself
that no one needs to know Granddad was born
in Iowa to a woman part Chippewa, or how our line
of the family got stuck in adolescence for 150 years
and no one remembers why. We couldn't go home,
and after a generation, we moved on—
to Oklahoma. You know how families go.

I crow that I am bringing the family back to forgive.
To Wisconsin, the land where the Presbyterian
Dickeys first loved and adopted America. I stop at
the antiques shoppe across the road from the water tower,
and walk in anonymously. I don't say too soon
my name is *Dickey* and become an instant celebrity.
I'm nonchalant. I ask how *Dickeyville* got its name.
They shrug. No one knows. A codger smokes a pipe,
rocks in the back corner next to a wooden Indian,
the spitting image of Uncle Elmer.
He asks if I have seen the famous Catholic Grotto
built here in 1930. *Son, you simply must.*

So, this town might as well have been called *Kieler,*
settled by the German Catholic, Johannes Kieler,
and named when son George opened a post office.
Or given the name of the ghost town *Burton,*
where Daniel Burt built a steamboat to navigate
to New Orleans. Or maybe everybody knew the story.

Dickeyville got its name like I did—at a church social
a man didn't plan to go to, the first man
a woman happened to marry, to keep their secret.
One thing though is certain. Whatever happened
in the 1840's, Wisconsin isn't talking.

HOLIDAY

The oxygen concentrator breathed
all night, played Mother
in the TV movie's starring role.
Next day about noon, we opened gifts,
and towards night we said goodbye.

Iowa. The turbines waved their arms,
begged us to return for gas and snacks.
The Kozy Shack stood still by the river,
but we were on the interstate by then,
going way too fast past the farms.

Wind and dead uncles grow crops,
and Dad makes a plywood boat
to cross the creek—with new tools
I'd given him for Christmas. They say
the fishing across it is always fine.

COMING HOME TO SEE DAD

The fields are still, full of the sorrow of sparrows.
A few migratory birds winter in the windbreaks.
They know the snow will melt and move on,
the land soon warm enough for the population.

Once governed by the summer sun, I broke up
the clods like daily bread. My youth talked silly.
Dirt clumps were clogged sentences. I said it once,
heard the hired hands laughing in the hayloft.

Dad had his own way about words, folks
and things. He respected every tool. Everything
inhabited its own place. God took care of fools.
His pencil stub calculated the very day to plant.

Last October, Dad and I sowed the green,
winter wheat. In what is now my eighty acres,
the images became metaphors, twisted and twined.
His hands worried, imagining his land as mine.

FAMILY FARM TOMORROW AT PUBLIC AUCTION

In the realty office, charcoal lines had stood
guard over the orange farm. Driving home,
he squinted at the artist's pencil rendering,
recognized each tree, each brother.

Ghosts with family resemblances inhabited
the shadows: abandoned cars, the tractors
boys once explored along the snow fences.
The sky—counted on for years—disappeared.

At home, his wife turns off the room's switch.
In darkness, his eyes learn again to see:
the curves of the heritage bedpost
he might be able to afford to buy back.

He listens to the creaks and groans of the lonely
house in bad weather soon to be haunted.
He thinks about all that may happen
tomorrow. She spreads the comforter.

They lie in their bed a last time. All being,
they wear not a stitch of clothing but time.

ON THE STATE LINE

Whiskey asses hang half off the bar stool.
Belt buckles are brighter than wits.
Moons leer all over the angels' tits.
The fields were wet when he was in school.

Filipino girls blur and fade on his forearm,
strip bills from a frayed wallet. In dry dock,
battleships rust. Not lonely now, he'll knock
up opportunity, drive home to his father's farm.

THIS P-EM CAN'T EVEN FIX THE LEAKY FAUCET

Don't get me wrong. Poems do a number of things. Once in a while, they get you love after hours at Goodtime Charlie's. In Europe once, it is said they monitored whether the trains were running on time. They built nations and resurrected ancient cultures out of physical ruin. Lately, there has been a huge market demand for them. Or should be, if there wasn't a lack of a knowledge of history in the Pentagon. Poems create gods but embarrass them. They can help you tell one tombstone from another, say your grandfather's from the one of the town librarian whom he never left Grandma and married. Let's face it though. They cannot do everything. I don't know what more to tell you.

Any problem worth its salt is unbearable, Grandma used to say. Her soldier was away at war and Grandpa had walked into the dime store. Her sister had something incurable. I could go on, but I can't. Did I get at least one right? Myself, you ask? My wife and I have irreconcilable differences, differences that divorce don't fix and wouldn't fix if all 6.2 billion people stood in line all day at the courthouse and got divorced for us.

I scavenge through the dusty, bottom drawers of the antique bureaus in the attic. Yes, the ones I sold years ago at a flea market. That is where I find the essential things that keep all things going: secret prayers for lost soldiers and poems that whisper nothings in our ear, after hours, and faithfully, lovingly, respectfully can't solve anything.

LAZARUS, VISITING KANSAS

So he called to him, 'Father Abraham, have pity on me and send Lazarus to dip the tip of his finger in water and cool my tongue, because I am in agony in this fire.

—Luke 16:24 (KJV)

When she runs out of people to visit,
she visits the headstones. There is family
all along I-70 from Salina to Hays—
Uncle Rudy with his shirt off in the fields
plowing on his John Deere. That day
in 1966, Aunt Betty wouldn't stop
to give him a drink of water for the way
he looked. He didn't appear a good
Christian man and certainly no brother
of hers. Today she would donate a thousand
bucks to hell to give him a drink of water,
make him the richest man in the family
no longer alive. Her back stooped, she pours
water as if out of her eyes, to fill the vase
and keep alive the goldenrod and tansy
she clipped by the roadside. And off she goes
to visit Aunt Ruth, not knowing anymore
whether the people are here or they're gone.

THE OLD-TIME HARDWARE STORE

Among the antiques and clutter of Meeske's,
Fred scrunches between the close aisles
of Weeping Water and local Nebraska history.
At the cash register, the dust covers candy bars.
Doorknobs were last priced twenty years ago.
Once by grasping the hardware just right,
if only it were installed, he could have walked
into a room that could have been his life.

On the sidewalk, the retired soldiers talk
six-man football before the districts coupled.
The patchwork clientele joke: *Fred has a nose*
for finding things. Like the holes
in Springfield's defense, he finds the light
fixture not made since 1986, the exact part
to repair a whatchamacallit bought in 1975.
The ladies know genius when they see it.

Fred today is helping Sally Lee Williams,
who graduated just one year behind us.
Every day it is something new with her.
Today she needs to match a color
from an old cloth. Fred pretends not to see
the paint-spattered arms he once touched,
nor think of university girls in Autumn.

Of course, she was Sally Lee Asner then,
and Fred had earned the right, taking her
to the prom and all. They even tried again—
five years ago. He tries not to remember
anymore. *Maybe she is in the middle of the job,*
he says to himself. He mixes a gallon
of semi-gloss, matches her paint on a stick.
Day in and day out, Fred then walks her up

the aisle. The brass-plated knobs, bought
once or twice but returned, refuse to rust.

THE NIGHT MY FATHER AND I LOST EACH OTHER

I just wanted to know something.
I climbed out of bed, crept to where
my father was sleeping. I said
I wanted water. He got up,

kissed Mother goodbye.
Out of the bedroom, through his den,
into the kitchen, I followed him to where
he found water dripping. We couldn't

go back to bed. I fell asleep
at the table. With a pipe wrench,
he was taking off the faucets. In a dream,
I heard my mother's voice.

A door slammed. I didn't know where
he was. In another, I awoke in a room.

INCIDENT NEAR O'NEILL, NEBRASKA

That new idea is truest which performs most felicitously its function of satisfying our double urgency. It makes itself true, gets itself classed as true, by the way it works . . .

—William James

The young man in the black mask
enters the farmhouse
like he is entering the family.
He is going hunting.
This is why he is carrying
a rifle and a knife.
The boys haven't put away
the baseball bats and gloves.
Jessica is on the phone.
Jessica is always on the phone.
Mom paces. She needs
to make a call.
The apple fritters
cool in the kitchen.
Jessica gets off the phone.
Jessica screams.
The young man in the black mask
does not know anymore why he is here.
Jessica screams louder.
The young man in the black mask
would rather be in church
this Sunday, not listening
to some silly girl scream
her head off all day.
He hadn't figured on this,
this morning when he

was feeling a tad lonely
and couldn't get his truck to start,
and decided to go hunting.
Nothing freaking works anymore,
he says. It's life. At any minute,
something terrible might happen.
Dad comes in from the fields
and recognizes Charlie
before it is too late—
Charlie, the neighbor's son,
whose head was never quite right—
Charlie, who in the fall
had gone off to the city,
to college, and to work.

A RENO COUNTY, KANSAS CHURCH CEMETERY

The farmers—archaic, or at least historic,
nod off in assigned pews with head rests,
exact location based on annual donations.
Stoic board members with iron-brown hands

governed the potluck suppers, rummage sales,
Wednesday night prayer meetings,
the budgeted and unbudgeted maintenance
projects. Not for a minute do they care

to pinch wives of 70 to 150 odd years
lying next to them, who still dream
of Sunday pot roasts and time with grandbabies.
It took a century to build this church,

and on nothing but faith, damn hard work,
and time no one had enough of. A sign
"First Lutheran Church Cemetery" groans
from its rust like it has for twenty years.

The only thing odd is the town drunk
from the nineteen thirties settling in clay
and loam in the back row. He got his plot
and burial when an unknown woman

burst into town, flashed nothing but makeup
and a smile (his only daughter it turned out),
and on the side, she slipped the temporary
reverend a brand new one hundred dollar bill.

SISTER LYONS AND THE GOSPEL

For the preaching of the cross is to them that perish foolishness; but unto us which are saved it is the power of God ... hath not God made foolish the wisdom of this world?

—1 Corinthians 1:18-20 (KJV)

Tuesdays at four on KRFM, she exhaled sacred texts
and metaphor. She discerned prophecy from rhyme.
Her voice was the Lord's mighty rushing wind,
huffing all God's news into 12 minutes, saving three
to close with a prayer in tongues. *Just to spite the Devil,*
she'd say. After school let out, I'd drive the 35 miles
to Newton and bring her home. In the car, Grandma
talked about biscuits and gravy, the things I understood.

How Grandpa said her name, it rhymed with glory:
Clorie has a calling from the Lord. He told me to stay
in school, then he split for heaven. She sold
the house that cost him 10 hours a day for 40 years.
She got 15 minutes a week for 6 months. Rather
than to take her home to another fight with Mom,
I wanted to eat biscuits and gravy in her kitchen
forever, to give thanks that the Lord's work and all
the foolishness wasn't broadcast to the Wichita I knew.

WHAT WISCONSIN TOOK

The maples are out of work this winter. On the state
highway lining the fields, the trees are stripped,
but create no new economies. The wind strums a guitar
that is badly out of tune. The corn men of Orfordville
with stubble faces drink their coffee black, parlay
excuses on hockey games, argue over an obsolete war
and a buzzer-beater goal thirty three years ago, wink
at the widowed waitress and a dad's Prohibition profits.
Somewhere else in town, the plump and skinny wives
crow of granddaughters with money and day jobs
in Milwaukee. Someone else's daughters have the night
jobs. The men could forgive their own, had the girls
not forgotten when they left what it took to make this life.

THE RADIO IN WARTIME

Her boys are headed back to the fields after the noon dinner. She yells after them. She just thought of something to say to Elmer. He always has a book in his hand while he's eating and don't pay her no never mind. *Elmer! Pigs do not sweat!* The hinges on the screen door need oil and squeal like hogs across the dirt roads of Eastern Oklahoma. She mutters, you can't believe everything you read. With the boys out of the house, she listens to the wireless through the static for the voices of Murrow and Roosevelt.

The washing must keep until tomorrow. This afternoon is canning and de-heading a chicken for supper. Or scooping a few bags of wheat grain out of the silo to sell. If her throat can take it. She allows herself nary a thought of this weekend's coming church social, or God forbid, the dancing and spooning that always seems to get started. She is a Christian lady and her James is in France, a place in the world she would nary of known from Oklahoma City if things were different somehow. But it's where her mind is transported every night when her day ends. She listens in the dry, dusty scoops of air for Murrow, Roosevelt, or perhaps Fibber McGee and Molly.

ii. A Knack For Losing Things

DEAN'S TREE SERVICE

Cuddling a cup of hot tea, a man's wife
scoots her chair from the kitchen table,
watches through a sliding-glass door.
By nine o'clock, the cherry-picker
is high in the broadleaf linden.
The man's arms hold a chain saw,
snap old and decayed limbs,
one by one that once protected
the house through years of weather.

Upstairs from the bedroom window,
her husband is surprised, had thought
the saw would need more horsepower.
His grandparents made this acreage
a homeplace—planted the shade,
planned soon to start a family.
She admires the man's arm strength,
how he knots the rope around each branch
just so, drops them with no damage
to the ground or to the neighbors' lines,

reducing the risks of a situation—
a broken fence or a child getting hurt.
She laughs as Dean answers his cell
in the high branch. She knows him,
and only she can know he is making
a dumb excuse about lunch to the girls
at the office. He flicks a cigarette
onto her yard. She seems happy.
Tomorrow he'll bring back a grinder
to clean out the stump and roots.

Her husband pays him what he asks,
though somewhat below the going rate.
A gentleman, he tells Dean he's done
a good job, one he himself could not do.

A KNACK FOR LOSING THINGS

The art of losing isn't hard to master.
—Elizabeth Bishop, "One Art"

What had been lost along the casual way
will not come back to me another day,
and to be frank, it often will not do
to keep a useful thing its use past due.

Whether a key, or say, a fountain pen,
the things I want today, I won't again.
Please, if I lose a button, don't advise,
because if I were but to realize,

I'd stop and stay behind too long to look
for what I might not find. The time it took
I could have used to buy a newer shirt,
not stoop to pick up what was claimed by dirt.

Every day the things desired are lost.
To get them back comes at a greater cost.

DEPARTURE

The snowflakes fell like all the others,
though they may as well be microscopic,
crushed bones. They cannot melt
even if the ground somehow forgives.
I watched the sun in its last hour
of color. You stood on the neighbor's porch.
The lights came on to greet you,
and the sunset followed you from room
to room, through the foreign household.

BREAKING INTO UNLOCKED HEARTS

He enters by the bedroom window,
he theorizes, that in loneliness
she may have forgotten to close.
The radio is on and the lights that would
be off, were someone at home.

He carries a knife, discovers the book
she was reading when she fell asleep.
He studies what she left of dinner.
The oven is left on. *Dear, you should*
take better care of yourself.

He must take something,
but not the cheap rings on her vanity.
She surprises him from the vestibule.
He is falling in love. Her bedroom
is the neighborhood where he

wanted to live all of his life.
They will sleep inside the purple
suburb past dawn and direct
the black and white choreography
of the children at breakfast time.

SOLDIER LEFT IN THE SAND

He came home along with the artifacts. But if he sleeps on the cot, his face folds flat still in full comportment. He was too young to prove to the reporter that he needed a shave. The microwave called home base was set for 145 degrees for 12 months. *I can fry bacon and scramble eggs in my helmet, SUH!* There was no telling what would happen leaving an innocent bag of popcorn in your backpack. Like at home, he hardly noticed the explosions at first. The risks and dangers of trying to make a game plan to go to college and making the old man say proud. Not every threat was a full mortar round or rocket-propelled grenades. If the recruiting Sarge said choice, how was it not true? *Son, don't say bacon. Remember where you are. Leave on the gawdamned helmet. You can be sniped picking up a child with your good arm in the alleys of this secured town.*

WOODS INTERIOR

After the charcoal on paper, Woods Interior (1905) by Robert Henri in the Sheldon Memorial Art Gallery, Lincoln, NE.

A boy's dreams strut big though small a place.
His pride grows tall as oaks from acorns stand.
Our son was young and so professed to know
the sun will spill its light above the leaves
as rays of paint so he can flaunt his chance.
He walked the trail with us, his pace the same

from tree to tree. The bark appeared the same.
He likely thought he'd walked all day in place
and all he'd seen was ruled by nature's chance,
and not by will. Given the time, he'll stand
as tall as mothers can. So when she leaves,
he'll know (though nothing tells him how he knows)

his time has come. Who taught him how to know
such things? He'll want her gone, not be the same.
"It's up to me, he'll say, to turn the leaves
of my own book, to read and mark my place."
A son's mistakes his parents must withstand.
One day he'll turn from us. We'll learn by chance.

Our careless talk that day gave him a chance
to run a path we could, of course, not know.
The marsh did not afford the ground to stand.
Through not a thought-out plan though all the same,
the steps he chose soon put him in a place,
where random nature's orders gave him leave

to march like Majors wearing shoulder leaves.
The light began to fade. He forced the chance,
desperate to escape to anyplace.
Night comes quick is what he'd start to know,
and nothing seems the same that is the same.
Confused at first, but he must understand

that one must draw a line on which to stand.
If lost in evening sky and all light leaves,
no one can see which shadows are the same.
Above the trees, the sun withdrew all chance.
He saw what I could not afford to know—
that aged trees once giants stoop in place

for younger trees to stand. We took the chance
to leave him be, to learn what he must know
in time—or lack of same—to stand his place.

INSTRUCTIONS FOR BUYING A LOAF OF BREAD

Walk down the stairs quietly.
Your father may be napping
on the couch. Talk about
getting married.
Drive by the church. Make it
real. Make sure you have
the exact change.
Don't slam the door
or lose the house key.
You may need to get back in.
Pick a good neighborhood.
Walk a dog.
Don't go out after dark.
Make sure you have
the exact change.
The saved and the lost live
on every street between
here and there. Be wary
if the man says he wants
nothing but you.

FAILED PORTRAIT OF THE ARTIST'S DAUGHTER

Her face does not haunt us,
as it did in the early work.
In the Mosaic period, her eyes
and mouth blurred together
in color beyond and within
the surface—as irises reflecting
the tales of tongues. This now
seems an unfinished canvas—
the nose, the lips stamped.
You think this cannot be true.

Whether she is beautiful is not
the issue, or if her father left
her mother to paint nudes
in a warmer studio. He has somewhere
to go this afternoon. In a hurry,
he forgot something. His own life
he keeps from the canvas. The critics
explain that the master craftsman,
short of finances, needed to produce
a hundred daughters in an afternoon.

LAST CALL, LAST CHANCE FOR CARELESS LOVE

Accidentally, I left a couple of words I should have said in a steamy hotel room in Savannah. Foolishly, I called back and asked: Can housekeeping retrieve something and ship it to me exactly as they find it? I left my passion for our music on a bench outside a century-old auditorium in Nashville. It must have been tossed out with the pizza box we shared that once-in-a-lifetime night in New Orleans singing with the Delta Jazz Band. I can't hardly want to get that back.

I misplaced the sure fire #1 chart hit that we had worked on for months—in airports, hotels, concert halls—while the snow sang harmony for us in Buffalo, the sun stayed up all night in Vegas, and the rain snookered us that closing night in Memphis.

All I know is that when the bellhop asked if the limo keys you left with the concierge were what you planned to quit the tour and live with, I lied and told him that the show was only meant for the one night, I winked, or maybe a whole weekend if I got lucky. He suggested that maybe if the backing vocalists in the farewell concert tonight hit the right note exactly on time with the bass and fiddle like they have no clue how to do, there won't be a dry eye in the hall.

HOW THE LOVERS BECAME DIFFERENT

Some nights they could not sleep.
At one point about midnight,
their words took on a meaning.

And he couldn't say she was right,
and he couldn't say she was wrong,
so he said, you can say that again,

and she did and she began to believe it.
She had a thesis. She found evidence:
the books became dog-eared,

the key verses highlighted, unreadable
notes got scrawled into the margins
from lunch with professors

and colleagues. He stopped asking
for proof. The explanations stretched
long and tedious. She was convinced,

by the very authority of God.
In time, love and logic excused
themselves from the discussion.

SHOPPERS

She is fourteen, not yet
anything, known
to classmates by a twist
to the mouth or nose.
One in particular, a boy,
is fascinated but withdraws.
Let us hope he is not
obsessed with the beauty.
There is a dogfight
between her boyfriend
and her best friend—
Parmenides vs. Heraclitus—
Being versus Becoming.
Others in the school
of friends float as fishes.
They too have become known,
demonstrate a genius
for the fashions, an expertise
on styles just months ago
weird, gross.

The Braces sport tattooed waists.
Jeans hang below the equator.
The Platonic Security Guards
note that all we observe
in our universe is change,
ask where permanence,
the true source of happiness,
derives. Newton advises: a body
in planetary motion must remain
in motion, even when it laughs
or sneers. Metal in all the places

makes everything personal,
and not possible, in the mall
where the past, present, and future
of our good earth come fully into play
and everything on the shelves
is there for no reason
other than it has not been bought.

A THIEF WE BARELY NOTICED

A thief is living with us,
tearing shreds of wallpaper,
pulling threads from the carpet.

Every night it is the same.
Footprints wear the linoleum.
Luster is stolen from the silverware.

He sculpts your face and hands
after his image, chips away
the flesh he no longer desires.

I can't take it anymore.
In the family room, he claims
his full share of an old man's

last air. I am calling the police.
But it doesn't matter. Already,
you left me for his paradise.

HOW TO DECORATE A CLOSET

Throw out all your good clothes
that allow yourself to be seen in public,
all the shopping bags that could be tied
to objects with marketable value.
Stacked in piles, they lean against
the vacuum as if something is there.
Give away anything someone may
accidentally find. You require the space.

Express a style largely—as in a ballroom,
as though the space affords ballrooms:
golden, flowing curtains, Stein ways,
murals, white furniture, plush carpets.
You may fall asleep here, have dreams
you will not allow yourself to wake from.
Allow yourself to wonder if you
could have made different choices.

Find the art that will satisfy
the most rebellious spirit, one not
to share with spouses or murderers.
Let it contain everything you can't,
no, won't explain even to close walls.
This is where amateurs like you and I
hang our masterpiece. Shut the door
tightly. You will not be alone.

GIRL IN BIKINI, BY THE WATER'S EDGE

The shadows try hard not to look lonely.
Under the clear surface of the pool,
they bend images of sky. Nearby,
softball lights are only in it for the beauty.
She splashes her feet at poolside,
disturbs the stars. No parent can tell her
grace does not call attention to itself.
She thinks the scene is all about her—
the way she wraps in the towel, the way
she opens it. Unbeknownst to her,
the stars dance in the water
if I squint enough, and even bodies
reflect beauty where she loses all her faults
in the cuts and the angles of the water.

CAUGHT UP IN A MOMENT

Last night, we heard the paparazzo's
camera pop. It took us back
ten, twenty, fifty years—through
hip-hop, acid rock, jitterbug.
The song that happened to play
one night still was playing, the night
everything and nothing became
clear, as if one idea at a sidewalk cafe
could change life's direction.
What climbed uphill eventually
slowed, and before you knew it,
caught the opposite drift. I swore
I detected the scent of a cigarette
leaving. A blind man walked by
with a sax. The famous woman
in the black dress in question
waited for a taxi. The most casual
glance took on an ominous note,
although nothing at first warned
any of this had happened to us.

AT THE LAST MINUTE, BEAUTY ESCAPES STARDOM

Beauty, the boys can't take their eyes off you. They got you in the cross-hairs, in the sights, trying everything they got—the false lashes, the meter, the eyeliner, the rhyme. They take a little practice with a target pistol, write a love ditty to you and the little sis Art, but our real business—don't forget, is crime, cosmetics, and bullets.

We'll let her go. Scram kid get out of here. Shake that booty. Tell Mama Sis might not be home for dinner. Don't mess with us, Beauty. You're ours. You're too far in bed with this thing. We own you. You are what we came for. If we can't have you, no one else will. We're aiming Colt 45 millimeters at your head. Only lucky for you, beauty doesn't last forever.

(IT COULD) HAVE GONE EITHER WAY

It could have gone either way. The moon
was dripping alphabets, on the one hand.
On the other, she was saying:
We can be friends. I can get married again
and put the children in a private school.
You will have all day to do—
whatever it is you do.
I appreciated the concern, but the truth was
I hadn't done anything. We didn't know why
other people get *so* so about daily affairs.
Everything would be better for all concerned.
We didn't mention what we'd do
with the children's first alphabet, or our old
high school's moon. If we had, we might not
have known how it all would have turned out.

TEA AND COFFEE

My wife's study group
constructs itself on the veranda,
drinking tea and Bible topics.
Tonight they are doing Ruth
for the third time.
At least, I think it is tea.
Maybe they are drinking
the sad wisdom that only comes
from ages and ages
of drinking tea.
The leader reads scriptures,
dips the leaves into the water—
all sea, ocean, and river.

They are lovely ladies,
or at least they once were.
But now they drink tea.
They did not always drink tea.
One in particular, I know
for a fact, drank beer.
I am drinking coffee—
which to be fair,
I did not always drink—
and see the one I once knew
distracted by bluebirds
in the limbs of the red oak
doing God knows what.

The ladies have become known
as serious drinkers of tea,
will stand transfixed
at the grocery aisle,
reading and selecting labels—
the teas God would have them drink:
from Constantinople,
the Holy Lands, or Peking,
and then come home
with a tea from America,
a tea they can explain—
to husbands, to the other ladies,
a tea they could afford.

PEBBLES

In the middle of love
there was a large stone.
Soon there were little pebbles
all over. What was once
a green valley was
becoming a rocky hillside.
There was one thing to do,
but we could not bear it.
Rather, we bought
wine buckets at great cost,
gathered the small pebbles
and collected them
one small bucket at a time.

We pounded the large stone
with hammers.
It made more pebbles
of which we were always proud
and we carried them away
to a place by the church
and by the river. Through all,
the stone remained large.
By time the sun was down
and the day was done
and the moon was up,
there were more pebbles
than before.
But we were tired then,
and we lay down.

iii. We Never Know

THE MEN'S HOT TUB AND THE FEAR OF THE UNKNOWN

He looks human enough, but in the times of breaking news, I do not know if to speak to the guy. I may be totally wrong about it. I read his face to determine whether something hides under his bed and being a patriot like myself, he must fight against the evil with every word of the Constitution he can muster, even if violently. He can't worry about that anymore. From the distance of 100 feet, I hear the murmur and the innuendo of the cable news network other than the one I watch all the time not rise to the level of sense, and thus sound compelling. I fear the man may be listening to it and doesn't want to be my brother. He hates totally different things, I suppose. I cannot suggest even for a laugh—"At least, there are no bombs in the water," although both of us know there are none. Perhaps his bombs that don't exist are redder than mine. As he leaves me in the tub, he says he's tired, been tired all day. And I agree with him and smile. I hardly anymore have the energy to think myself. And that is when he went to the locker, retrieved an object, and came back and fired the gun at me.

HAPPINESS AND SADNESS YOU WILL NOT HAVE WITH YOU ALWAYS

However big you are today, tonight you will be nothing.
The moon and the stars will defeat you in a simple game
of chess, although you tell them—once you
had wealth and a lovely wife. They will demand
from you a bottle of your finest wine. From the cellar,
you cannot return. Thieves have turned the wine
into water. Flashlights search for you through the tunnels.
Voices will call out your name, even echo for a time
in the stadiums, but you have lost any claim to speech
or to hearing. Though small you are tonight, tomorrow
you will be everything. The raindrops will make
room for you between the cobblestones of the avenues.

THEORIES OF FAMILY

The family consisted of one adult male,
one adult female, coconut cream pies,
a cache of ten 12-paks of Dr. Pepper
in the garage, my sister when not dating
the tattooed biker, Dad's Bible, and me.
Dad despised grades lower than a B plus.
We loved our enemies but sauerkraut
was not permitted in the house, nor folks
named Freud or Darwin, even if they lived
down the block and approached the steps
with a book as black and serious as
the Bible. More than anything, we feared
the theories of family running loose
in the neighborhood. One in particular
was two adult females, the loud music,
hugging and kissing friends in the yard.
One family was even named Beers.

TWO FAMILIES, ONE HOUSE

A young couple, and by the way, the nicest couple you would ever want to meet and one that we all agreed had earned the finest things in life were about to move into the neighborhood. It was whispered they had survived a holocaust where they had once lived. They survived, it was said, by believing years ago the landlord had promised them this one specific house for all of time, the one overlooking the vineyard. They had been cautioned. However, it might need to be rented to others until they could arrive. There might have been many empty homes in the neighborhood. That was not clear. The neighbors argued about it all the time.

One night, in the very middle of the night—one might even say, the midnight hour (and many do) a good man awoke from a nightmare. A family was moving into the home where he and his wife had lived for many years, raising their many sons and daughters. Perhaps in his imagination, perhaps not (though no less real), he feared from the ruckus that the young man and woman who had come in unannounced might be trying to have children in the other bedroom.

Not knowing what to say to them if they should come out of the bedroom to lounge around his kitchen table and try to get a little peace, the man opened the drawer of the nightstand for a cigarette and found an ancient weapon. In accordance with the holy commandments of his God and the ancestors, he called all of the sons together even the children and asked what they would have him do.

THE SEASON OF ALMOST

Almost by the hour
the red oaks
change clothes from green
to gold to gone.

The busted acorns spread
an oak floor
in tongue and groove,
snap and creak like a bed.

A hunter scurries, collects
his last pleasures
and needs.
Autumn achieves

its waiting for winter.
Anything and everything
seem almost
worth the dying for.

THE AWARDS CEREMONY

I was a cloud of no particular consciousness. Champagne glasses tinkled like Christmas bells. All the faces were huge and austere and resembled card-board posters. A political expert from India, a distinguished black man from television, and a woman of unquestioned scholarship and horn-rimmed glasses expressed a sense of humor I could not understand. They spoke passionately and intimidatingly. They spoke directly to me, or so I thought, but they seemed not to expect me to answer. They praised me in a language that I could not understand but which sounded commercial. I knew they all were very famous and I too now had become so. After they presented me with the award and a big check, they introduced me to the master songwriter of whom I had been a fan for fifty years. He closed the event with a song that he did not write, the song with which they always close the event. He said he liked my book, but anything I could say to him would be pointless. He asked if I would like to go with him to the recording studio. There he sang a song of bottomless darkness in my own words. He proclaimed that we had a #1 hit and he had achieved the expected sense of passion and dignity with it. The dude's eyes twinkled like a glass of bubbly.

THE OVENBIRD TODAY IN PROFESSOR ROGERS' BACKYARD

Ben got several good looks today
at the ovenbird in his backyard.
He said it was quite a sighting
from the deck and clearly a life bird—
"a little warbler with a jaunty tail."
He chuckled to see the web page online
depicting the bird's song with words:
"cher, tea-cher, tea-cher, tea-cher."
Ben had taught Analytic Philosophy,
and knew well what words can
and cannot do. The site went on:
Ovenbirds are known to sing together.
One bird starts. The second joins.
They pause, then sing. One and the other,
back and forth, for up to forty songs,
as if a single bird sings alone.
Not often understood is that ovenbirds
rarely interrupt the mate. Ben studied
under the students of Wittgenstein
and Russell at Cambridge and recalls
the Great Conversation with his students
in which he had made his living.

THE MEANING OF TOM

So on we worked and waited for the light.
—E. A. Robinson, "Richard Cory"

My friend Tom likes to hike.
You may have seen him
on the open road yourself.
He calls it walking his acreage.
He tells me it is not depression.
I believe him. Tom has no job
because he is a rich man.
He walks the Big Blue River
at midnight without a flashlight
just to see if he can do it.
He walks the state highway
to Manhattan until someone
returning from work gives him
a ride home. He asks them
to drop him off a mile short,
so they won't see how he lives.
Last week he did 21 miles,
a record for him.
Or five miles from the estate,
he camps in his motor home
at Turtle Creek State Park
before going home to the wife.
He says he wants to be with her
all day in their lovely home,
as you would if you didn't need
your job. He has his work.
In the spring, he may bike the state
down I-70, a fundraiser for the Lions,
if he can get the press coverage.

It is not depression, though
even I at first thought it was.
Of course, seeing him on the road,
you'd not know he is the rich man.

WINTERING AT BOYS TOWN

The public is not to be told. No curb
lines the brick streets to park the cars.
The neighborhood wants to be a suburb.
Let the gawkers drive to DeSoto Bend

and stare with binoculars on a rocky ledge.
The truth though, there are Canada geese.
The nuisance wildlife swim the lake's edge
near the newly-built Admission Center,

the birds skidding on the islands of ice
as to form a line. No boy or girl loiters
in the yards today. In the pricey
homes, the arms fidget under the desks,

solve algebra problems before being excused
for dinner. Elsewhere, winter was colder.
I am late for dinner myself, confused
by the working day's knowns and unknowns.

Fifty miles from DeSoto, down the flyway,
I stop to watch the ad hoc refuge. Geese flap
wings close-up, test the air, prep to glide away,
swoop to the adjoining corn—

only yards from the water's welcome,
and for the nourishment of the grit and the grain.

DESIGN

On his quiet, evening drive home, the dark, steamy suburbs rose from the manholes and extinguished the city. A sliver of a moon grinned at him in the rear view mirror. The man had emptied his life into the job today so when arriving home, his wife would pour him the glass of wine. She would greet him at the door, as if she had seen—not the Ghost in the Machine—but whatever it was she saw in him yesterday and the days before that. At the dinner table, the son - while not speaking anymore, may be reading nothing but a book of sullen, 19th century Russian fiction. The chicken teriyaki tells a joke without the taste to warn him that his life is done.

He cannot tell his wife where he went for lunch. His colleagues had scoffed at the snuff film's scene that held him too intimately for a professed, casual affair. He says to himself that if this were all meant to be, it would be called Design and Hume would have had no need for Darwin to fill in the cracks. God would be God and we all would be pocket-protected, student engineers. Slam Bam. The stars would punch out the cardboard sky into a pattern as Ptolemy surmised. The man's son's eyes would not be prisoners of 17th century time. The skyscrapers would not be the candles on Descartes' writing desk pleading to be snuffed out after the night of philosophical study.

WALKING ON WATER

Ripples slosh over your ankles, trying
to wash you up, say what can't be done.
Those nearest to you do not want you
to take the risks. They are wrong.
There is no reason the color of water
cannot be the same as a skyway.

Do not be distracted if your image
drops below the surface. It is not you.
It is a shadow. Forget all the sounds
that brought you here and now
leave you. You lost everything—
the ground under your feet.
It will not be found beneath a body

of water. Each day, be new.
Take one step before another, expect
the dust to accumulate underfoot,
slowly. Let whatever wants to be green
grow beneath you. Sometimes you may walk
with a pause, but there is no reason to fall,
until you come to the end of the river.

HYMNS SUNG FOR THE OBVIOUS

They call at all hours of the morning.
Were you awake? Uncle Fred. His heart.
One time it was our friend Julia.
So we made advance arrangements
for everyone that we have known.
At the hospice house, we tell the nurses
they don't need to call until
after breakfast. But even total strangers go.
The phone rings. It's 1 a.m. 2 a.m. 3 a.m.
This morning it was 2:49. *It's Fritz Faulkner.*
You played dominoes with him once.
We thought you would want to know.

THE MOMENT IT HAPPENS

We knew the moment it happened,
the exact moment the butter knife
dropped to the floor. We thought
maybe it would not have,
if only we had said the right thing.
All the family had come to sit
at the oak dining table,
but still away in their travels.
Not knowing what to say,
the children asked: *did the cuckoo stop?*
I looked at my sister.
My wife looked at my brother.
They looked back.
Mother never looked back,
turned to Dad who was not there,
proceeded to tell him about
the neighbor's rosebush,
the family that lives there no more.
Remember? They live across the street.
Oh Jack, you never listen to me.

FATHER'S BATTERIES

Father insisted always on having his own way. He wouldn't wait for his watch or even a CD player to run down before replacing the batteries. On a fixed schedule every three months, he changed every battery in the house, even the flashlights in the garage that would be needed in an emergency—just to make sure that none would fail at the precise moment he was stressed out, was wanting to hear his favorite song from forty years ago, or was shaving and getting ready to take Mom out to dinner. He said it was the only way to do things. Maybe I could learn a thing or two. That was before his heart attack, and all I could muster was annoyance and speculation why the tedious activities of the day wore him down so quickly.

THE END OF DAYS

So fare thee well my own true love
When I return united we will be.
It's not the leaving of Liverpool that grieves me
But my darling when I think of thee.
—"The Leaving of Liverpool" (Irish traditional)

It was there in the way light entered
the room, how the cold collected.
Dust on the bureau left a fingerprint.
There must have been a rustling

curtain upstairs, a noise I was not
sure I heard but could not forget.
Poppa came home singing
Fare Thee Well, My Own True Love.

Momma shut off the radio listening
for news of earthquakes, the Anti-Christ,
praying under her breath
for the Rapture to save her boys,

before the beast stumbled up the steps,
into her bed. He cracked the door to say
Goo'night Jamie, Goo'night Danny O,
and I knew soon I'd find his whiskey.

FOR A TIME

I was the one who lived to tell
the stars felt near, I shoveled snow.
The last I knew my friend was well,
I was the one who lived to tell.
Over the hill, I heard a bell.
For still a time the wind might blow.
I was the one who lived to tell.
The stars felt near. I shoveled snow.

HOW THEY ONCE WERE

Nothing reminds an old man how days
once were as do the melon-delicious
girls poolside—only a few inches
here and there shy of nakedness.
Only now, they stare and undress him:
Who gave him the right?
Though the boys in the locker room
for whom the girls might consider
giving up the last few inches,
seasoned to taste, speak of them,
as if the buffet were open all night.

AGING MAN HAS FLING WITH MATHEMATICS

He couldn't go home again to the old equation. Perhaps the solution was a return to the algebra of puberty? For years, he had calculated the unknown x in faces of the women in a choir, or the waitresses at a bar: m plus one unknowns in m equations.

Tonight he discovers the Zen of magic squares. Horizontally, from one nipple to the other, drawn string taut, down from the neckline to the leg, or diagonally from the right armpit to the left ankle—all lines add up to the same number, not this time one plus one equals two, or the limit as n approaches zero or infinity. There is a theorem. He trusts she will prove it.

RICK OF FIREWOOD OUT BACK, BEHIND THE NURSING HOME

In the back lot, the bark rots away from limbs,
the home for silverfish and cantankerous beetles.
Boys playing in the alley no longer hide
from mothers behind the dank log pile.
In the wet and dry stammers of forgetful weather,
the mind's full snow of eternal moments,
the heartwood loses tissue, all the evidence
of once being a tree among other tall trees
in a busy forest. Christian men brought the load,
mixed proud names of hardwood—oak, ash, maple—

fully seasoned and stacked to the proper angle,
the fiber brittle as a box of foxed
newspapers read daily. The men felt good
about what they had done. The young counted
their deed a service, asked only a fair wage.
The labor of course was appreciated, though
the firewood was not used, its time not come.
If now brought to the fire, the logs couldn't sustain
a night of conversation, would burn up in minutes,
crackling and popping as little, human voices.

I DON'T KNOW HOW SHE LEARNED OF SADNESS

I don't know how she learned of sadness.
Our curriculum was always joy.
When we lost all her houses, she lived
well enough in mine. When we quarreled

over nothing, it reminded us how things go.
The children came by the house to leave—
bringing babies into and out of each day.
Nothing got lost longer than the length

of a memory, while autumn returned
everyday to claim the paper loud leaves.
They cackled in the wind, whispered
behind our backs we were getting older.

All of this got out to the neighbors
who, one by one, observed the children
no longer coming to the front door
in the SUVs too early in the morning.

A RETIREE PONDERS HIS DAY

The morning has many rooms. He could do what he always wanted, but then he could do it tomorrow. In the attic, he imagines a dusty table that turns, spins a black dinner plate like a universe. A diamond pricks the darkness and the blackness orbits it. The steel arm tracks him from the first apartment to this house.

I should have known better
with a girl like you—

He listens to the scratches, the hisses, the pops that even now sound like the many years of himself. The afternoon has no walls.

SLIDING HOUSE

Magnitude 9.0 - NEAR THE EAST COAST OF HONSHU, JAPAN, 2011 March 11 05:46:24 UTC

My house floated—
like a Laysan albatross, Kyoko.
Above the world, it seemed,
and just for two minutes.
It sounds impossible.
If I had thought fast,
I'd first given you
everything I owned in it—
the photo of me with Akeno
at father's fish market.
If you could use it,
I'd offer you everything
I planned to cook
for the family dinner Sunday.
What a mess this is.
Mud and water,
chocolate and baking soda.
I will be okay,
even though I see my house
sliding and sliding
like a baseball runner,
into the Hirosegawa River.
And now, I must rest.
I might need your help
to pick up all the broken sticks.
There are more than all
the drops in the ocean.
I'll wait for you by the pagoda,
Kyoko, until your house
comes home from its sailing.

WE NEVER KNOW

what energy
burns in the light
across the road,
slips through the drapes,
or maybe borrows
light from our house.
And maybe there
is no motion of atoms
between the chairs
in the small room
of our neighbors,
as there is no
motion sometimes
between you and me.
We speak and laugh
almost daily
over fences.
There is light in
our eyes and when
it escapes, we know
we never knew.

CPSIA information can be obtained at www.ICGtesting.com
Printed in the USA
LVOW05s1923250813

349530LV00002B/140/P

9 781936 671205